PROMISED LAND.
THERE WITH YOU
KNOW TONIGHT T
WILL GET TO THE
AND I'M HAPPY,

For the foot soldiers of the movement—
past, present, and yet to come.

Ann Bausum

To my family, friends, and everyone else
who has inspired me . . . thank you.

Solomon Hughes

Reycraft Books
145 Huguenot Street
New Rochelle, NY 10801

reycraftbooks.com

Reycraft Books is a trade imprint and trademark of Newmark Learning, LLC.

Text © Ann Bausum

PRECIOUS LORD, TAKE MY HAND Words and Music by THOMAS A. DORSEY © 1938 (Renewed) WARNER-TAMERLANE PUBLISHING CORP. All Rights Reserved. Used by Permission of ALFRED MUSIC.

Reprinted by arrangement with The Heirs to the Estate of Martin Luther King Jr., c/o Writers House as agent for the proprietor New York, NY. Copyright © 1968 by Dr. Martin Luther King, Jr. Renewed © 1996 by Coretta Scott King.

All rights reserved. No portion of this book may be reproduced, stored in a retrieval system, or transmitted in any form or by any means, electronic, mechanical, photocopying, recording, or otherwise, without written permission from the publisher. For information regarding permission, please contact info@reycraftbooks.com.

Educators and Librarians: Our books may be purchased in bulk for promotional, educational, or business use. Please contact sales@reycraftbooks.com.

Sale of this book without a front cover or jacket may be unauthorized. If this book is coverless, it may have been reported to the publisher as "unsold or destroyed" and may have deprived the author and publisher of payment.

Library of Congress Control Number: 2023918654

Hardcover ISBN: 978-1-4788-8642-6
Paperback ISBN: 978-1-4788-8643-3

Photo Credits: Page 4A, 20, 24: DrPixel/Getty Images; Page 2B, 3A, 10B, 22B: Bettmann/Getty Images; Page 3B, 14, 30C, 31C: Randy Duchaine/Alamy; Page 3C: Abaca Carl Juste/Miami Herald/Alamy; Page 4B, 5A: Aqwees/Shutterstock; Page 5B: Eric Glenn/Alamy; Page 7: Mike Brown/Getty Images; Page 9A: William Warren/Alamy; Page 9B, 27A, 31D: Flip Schulke Archives/Getty Images; Page 10A, 11A: Sean Gardner/Getty Images; Page 10C: Morton Broffman/Getty Images; Page 11B: Charles Shaw/Getty Images; Page 11C: Granger; Page 13A: Entertainment Pictures/Alamy; Page 13B: TPLP/Getty Images; Page 15A: Martin Norris Travel Photography/Alamy; Page 15B: Walt Adams/Superstock; Page 17A: agefotostock/Alamy; Page 17B: Barney Sellers/USA Today Network; Page 18, 19B, 28, 30A, 31A: Hank Erdmann/Alamy; Page 19A, 26B: Andre Jenny/Alamy; Page 20A, 21A: Stephen F. Somerstein/Getty Images; Page 20B, 21B: Nathaniel Grann/The Washington Post/Getty Images; Page 20C: ipopba/Getty Images; Page 20D, 21C: Natalya Bosyak/Getty Images; Page 23B, 31B: Everett Collection Historical/Alamy; Page 24B, 25B: mwalton/shutterstock; Page 26A: Rolls Press/Popperfoto/Getty Images; Page 27B: TeddyandMia/Shutterstock; Page 30B: dcphoto/Alamy; Page 30D: Michael Ochs Archives/Getty Images; Page 31E: Glasshouse Images/Alamy; All other images from Getty Images

Author photo: Courtesy of Sam Boutelle
Illustrator photo: Courtesy of Solomon Hughes

Printed in Dongguan, China. 8557/0824/21501
10 9 8 7 6 5 4 3 2

First Edition Paperback published by Reycraft Books 2024.

Reycraft Books and Newmark Learning, LLC, support diversity,
the First Amendment and celebrate the right to read.

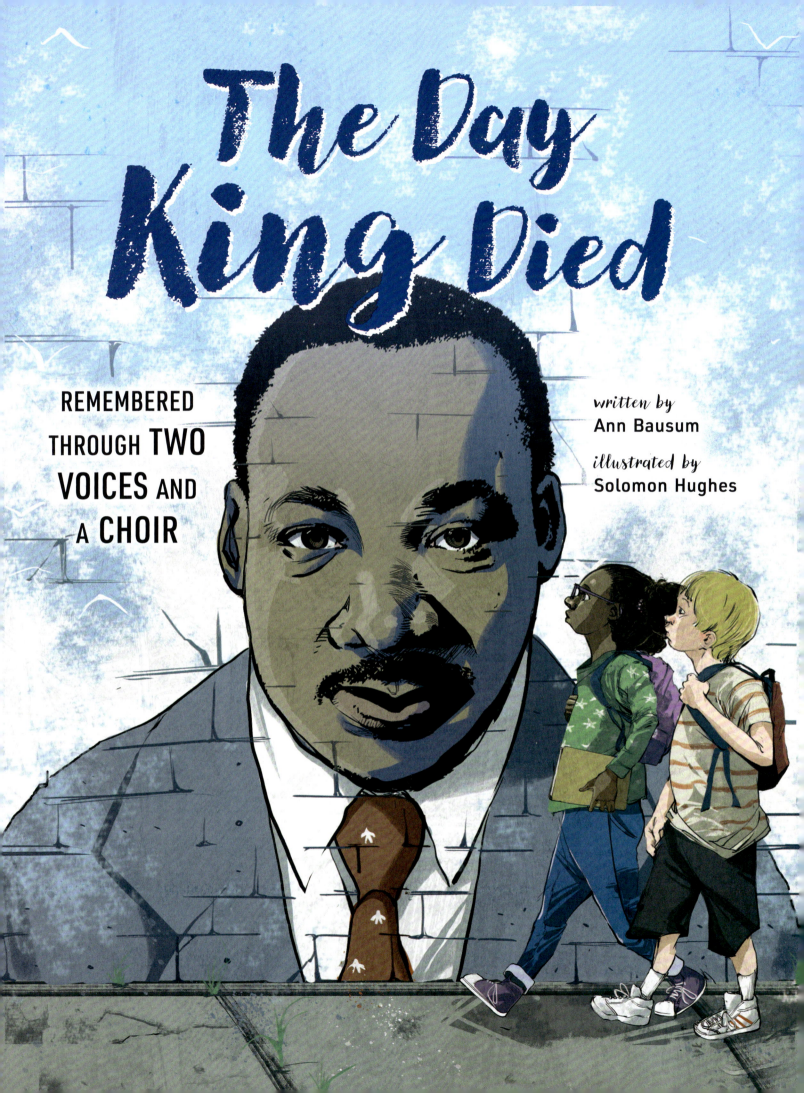

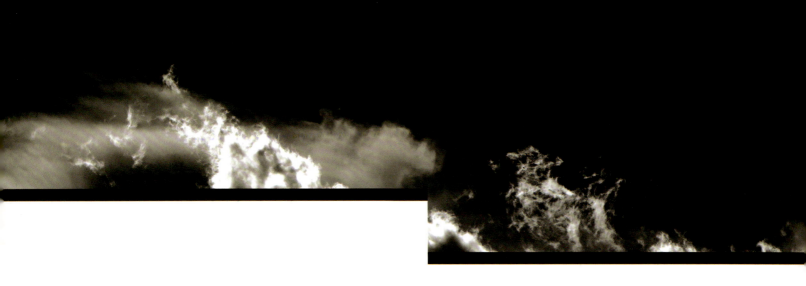

KING flew to town on troubled wings the day before he died. Memphis-bound despite a bomb threat.

Memphis-bound to help workers proclaim: **I AM A MAN.**
Memphis-bound on troubled wings the day before King died.

When my way grows drear,

Precious Lord linger near,

When my life is almost gone;

Hear my cry, hear my call,

Hold my hand lest I fall,

Take my hand, precious Lord,

lead me home.

KING entered the hall under thundering skies
the day before he died.

With a song in his head and a heart weighed with woe.

With a story of sights he'd envisioned below.

With
PROTESTS ALIVE

under thundering skies

the day before King died.

"Well, I don't know what will happen now.

We've got some difficult days ahead.

But it doesn't matter with me now.

Because I've been to the mountaintop."

King traveled to Memphis with **MARCHING SHOES** the day before he died.

SHOES SO POWERFUL his opponents tried to halt his feet.

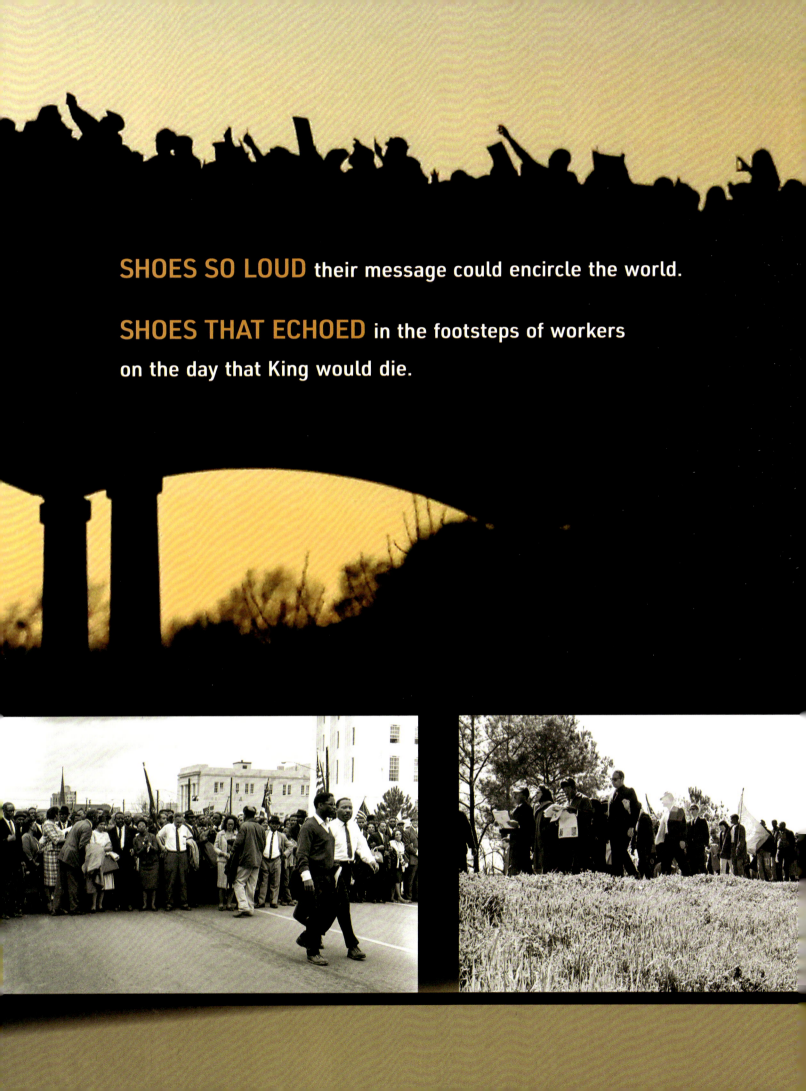

SHOES SO LOUD their message could encircle the world.

SHOES THAT ECHOED in the footsteps of workers on the day that King would die.

" And I don't mind. Like anybody, I would like to live a long life. Longevity has its place. But I'm not concerned about that now. I just want to do God's will. And He's allowed me to go up to the mountain. And I've looked over.

And I've seen the promised land. "

King stayed in his room under watchful eyes on the day that he would die.

The eyes of friends who talked, and sang, and played, and laughed together.

The eyes of hidden guards who spied unseen together.

The eyes of a killer who watched unknown all alone on the day that King would die.

" I may not get there with you. But I want you to know tonight, that we, as a people, will get to the promised land. And I'm happy, tonight. I'm not worried about anything. I'm not fearing any man.

Mine eyes have seen the glory of the coming of the Lord. "

King paused on the balcony at evening's edge
on the day that he would die.

The song in his head soothed the heart weighed with woe.
The song he shared with musicians below.

The song shots pierced at evening's edge
on the day that King would die.

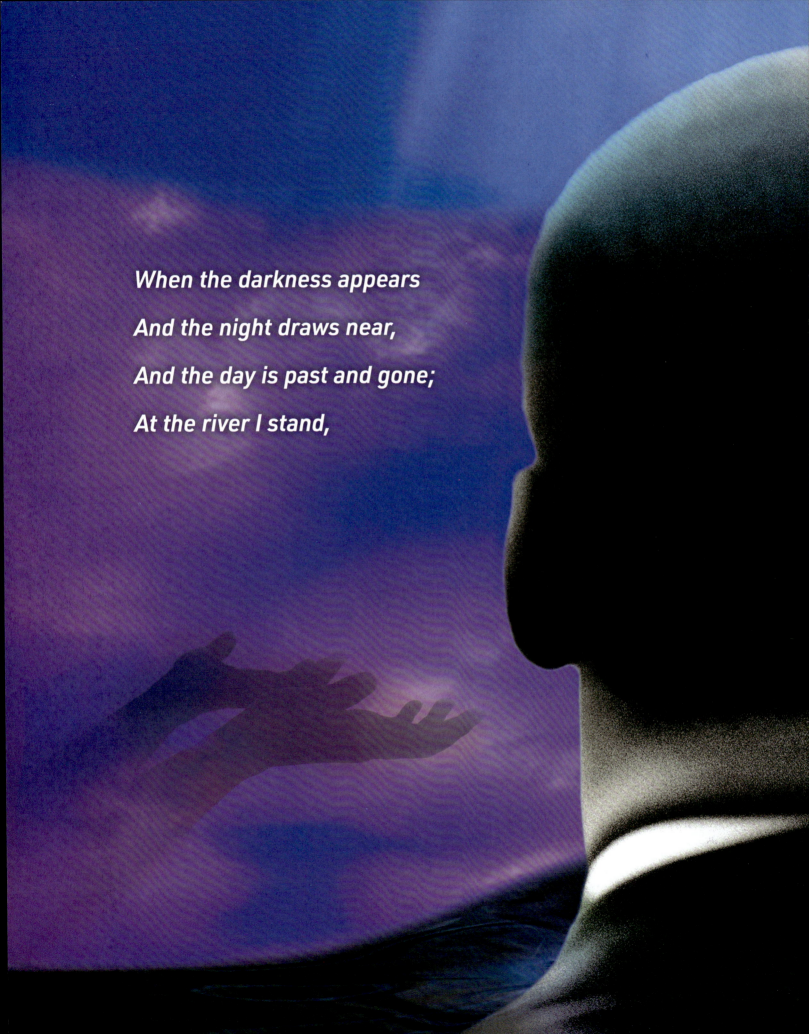

King refused to let hate consume his life on the day he died.

Cradled in love,
his wounds washed with tears.

Cradled in hope
for more love and less hate.

Cradled with faith
in hearts that beat

and marching feet on the day King died.

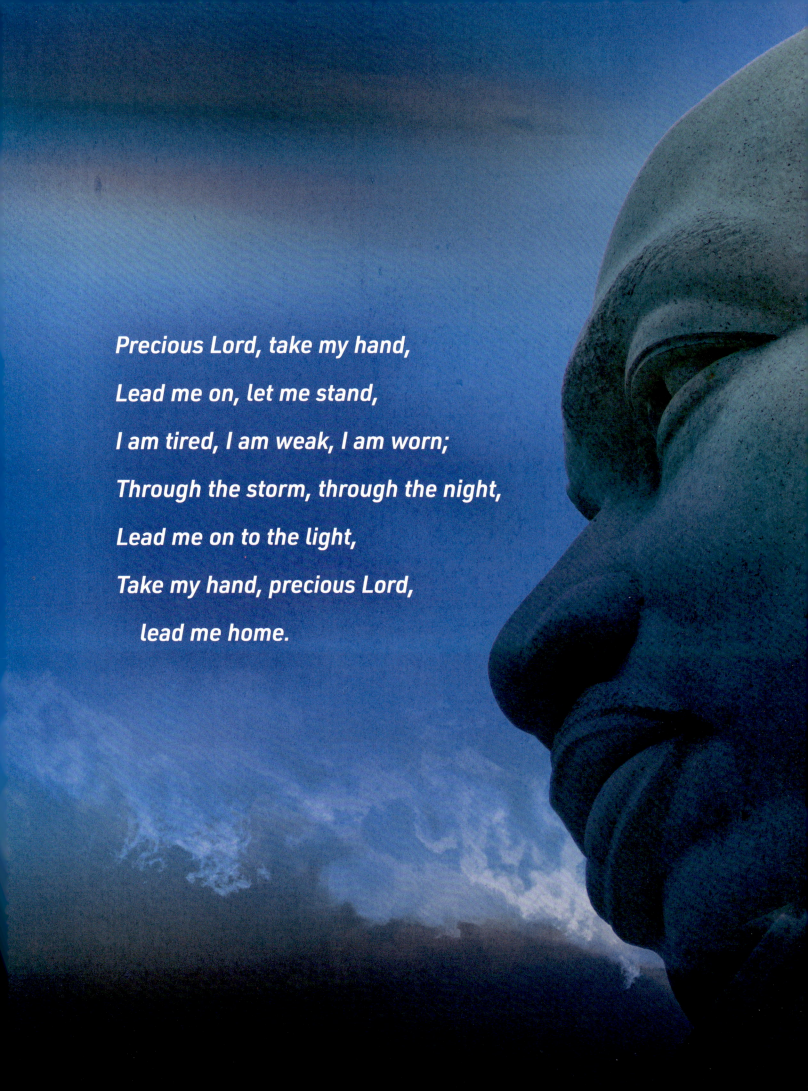

AUTHOR'S NOTE

It's important to remember that history is an attempt to make sense of events that unfolded in real time.

NO ONE KNEW when Martin Luther King Jr., flew to Memphis on April 3, 1968, that he was taking his final plane ride. **NO ONE KNEW** when he spoke that night at Mason Temple about having seen the mountaintop that he was giving his last speech. **NO ONE KNEW** that "Precious Lord, Take My Hand" would be the subject of his final conversation. **NO ONE KNEW** any of that until James Earl Ray fired those fatal shots as King stood on the balcony of the Lorraine Motel on the edge of evening, April 4, 1968. Barely an hour later, King was dead.

UNTIL THAT MOMENT
it had been just another day . . .

King's lawyers had gone to court to fight for his right to march in support of the city's striking sanitation workers. His allies had gathered to discuss strategies for the planned march. His best friend and aide, Ralph Abernathy, had shared catfish with him off a room service plate for lunch. His brother had visited, and they'd made a teasing phone call to their parents, pretending each was the other. His colleagues had joined him in a playful pillow fight after they'd gotten good news from court. All of them had listened to musicians practice for that night's rally in support of the strike.

King's assassin may have intended to stop King's push for change with his bullets, but bullets can't stop ideas.

One reason I've written two books about this history is to try to extend the understanding young people have of King beyond his oft taught "I Have a Dream" speech. We do King a disservice when we present him as a two-dimensional figure—the man with a dream—without emphasizing how he dedicated his life, and lost it, trying to turn this dream into reality. As King knew, having dreams is important, but dreams can be painfully difficult to bring to life and regrettably easy to quash. So he fought on.

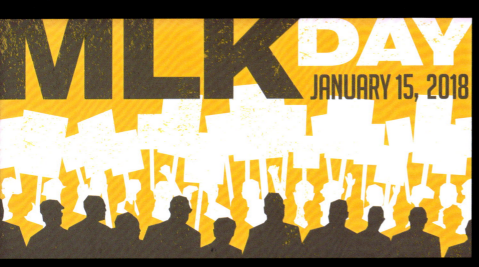

King's vision endures for a human family guided by respect and love. It echoes in the marching of thoughtful feet. It lives on in kindnesses offered to strangers. It pulses through the spirits of all who search beyond the surface to see the sparks of humanity that unite us regardless of how we look, what we believe, where we worship, whom we love, where we come from, or where

ABOUT THE BRAIDED TEXTS

I've interwoven my original text with two of the narrative threads that unfolded during the final hours of the life of Martin Luther King Jr.: the closing lines from the speech he gave the night before he died and the song that was on his mind at the time he was shot. Combined, I offer them as a unifying tribute to a life cut short, whether they are read as a single narrative or performed with two voices and a choir.

This braided approach is mirrored in the book's design, which blends original work by illustrator Solomon Hughes with historical images and photographic art.

KING'S "MOUNTAINTOP" SPEECH in Memphis rivaled any other address he made. He talked at length without notes. He told stories, praised the Memphis movement's fight for the striking sanitation workers, and recalled past attempts on his life. He spoke from his heart. People who heard the speech were moved to tears, and King himself became emotional as he concluded his remarks.

The second interwoven text comes from the gospel song **"PRECIOUS LORD, TAKE MY HAND."** Thomas A. Dorsey composed this song in 1932 after the death of his wife and infant son in childbirth. Years later in Memphis, King was asking musician Ben Branch to perform the song for him at their evening assembly. "Play it real pretty," he said. Then he was shot.

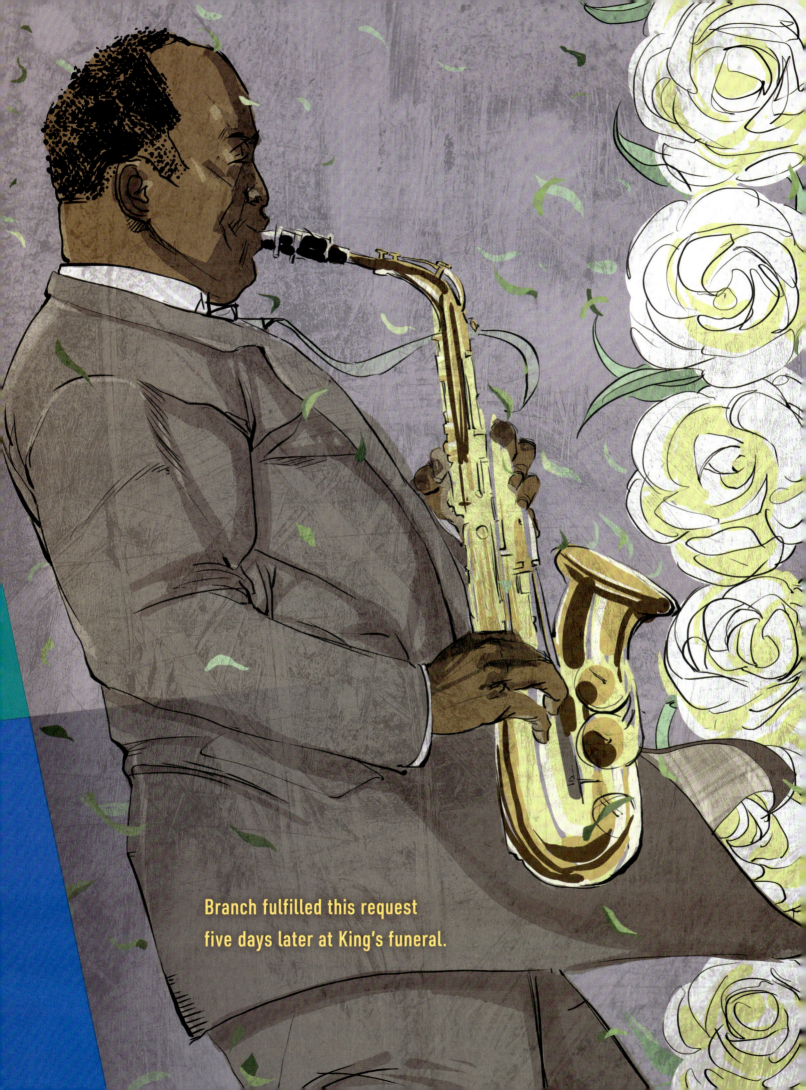

Branch fulfilled this request five days later at King's funeral.

BIBLIOGRAPHY AND RELATED READING

BIBLIOGRAPHY

Branch, Taylor. *At Canaan's Edge: America in the King Years, 1965–68.* New York, New York: Simon & Schuster, 2006.

Dorsey, Thomas A. "Precious Lord, Take My Hand." *Eternal Glory: Songs for Memorial Services.* Milwaukee, Wisconsin: Hal Leonard Corporation, 2005.

Honey, Michael K. *Going Down Jericho Road: The Memphis Strike, Martin Luther King's Last Campaign.* New York, New York: W.W. Norton & Company, 2007.

King Jr., Martin Luther. *I Have a Dream: Writings and Speeches That Changed the World.* Edited by James M. Washington. San Francisco, California: Harper San Francisco, 1992.

Sides, Hampton. *Hellhound on His Trail: The Stalking of Martin Luther King, Jr., and the International Hunt for His Assassin.* New York, New York: Doubleday, 2010.

RECOMMENDED VIDEO

"Thomas A. Dorsey: Precious Lord," audio history and a performance of the song. YouTube video: https://www.youtube.com/watch?v=zlmCflPD2s8

RELATED READING

Bausum, Ann. *Marching to the Mountaintop: How Poverty, Labor Fights, and Civil Rights, Set the Stage for Martin Luther King, Jr.'s Final Hours*. Washington, D.C.: National Geographic Society, 2012.

ANN BAUSUM was ten years old when she heard the news of the death of Martin Luther King Jr., announced on national TV. Years later, she wrote multiple books for young readers and teens about this and other pivotal events from social justice history, including the Freedom Rides of 1961 and the March Against Fear in 1966. Her work in Memphis for a book about the city's 1968 sanitation workers strike inspired this commemoration of Dr. King's final days. Having come of age in the American South, she lives now in southern Wisconsin.

SOLOMON HUGHES is an illustrator who has studied graphic design at Pratt Institute in his hometown of Brooklyn, New York. At age 8, his work had been displayed in the Guggenheim and, at 17, the Metropolitan Museum of Art. As an artist, he looks at works from the past and the present to expand his skills and craft. He currently lives at home with his parents, two sisters, two turtles, and one puppy.

I MAY NOT GET TH[ERE]
WANT YOU TO KN[OW]
WE AS A PEOPLE
PROMISED LAND.
TONIGHT. I'M NOT